Praise for
All I Need To Know
Manufacturing I Learned

D0446388

"If you're looking for an overview of current manufacturing concepts in an easy-to-read format, I suggest **All I Need To Know About Manufacturing I Learned In Joe's Garage**."
Jim Treece, Senior Correspondent
Business Week Magazine

"Excellent. Universally applicable to all manufacturing processes."
Robert A. Lutz, Vice Chairman
General Motors

"Refocused our organization on fundamentals of World Class Manufacturing."
Dale Philippi, Vice President
Eureka

"Simplest explanation of what it takes to achieve manufacturing excellence."
Training & Development

"Great easy reader - facilitates understanding of Lean Manufacturing concepts - highly recommended!"
Jon Enwiller, Lean Manufacturing Manager
AlliedSignal Aerospace

"Easy-reading book that gets the point across about JIT, lower inventories, and other aspects of agile manufacturing."
David Gardner, Director of Production
Maytag

"Really helped change the thinking in our manufacturing organization."
Mike Eagle, Vice President, Manufacturing
Eli Lilly

"Easy-reading book that will give you a quick education."
Design News

"A short course in lean thinking, told in reader-friendly style."
Donald E. Westerheide, Vice President
Lockheed Martin

"Wraps up more lessons in a one-hour read than all the high-priced seminars you could attend."
> John Guffey, Chief Executive Officer
> **Coltec**

"Perfect educational tool for production, sales, engineering - everybody!"
> Jack Farnandez, Director of Operations
> **Advanced Cardiovascular Systems**

"A story that includes all the lessons to become a world class manufacturing facility."
> Don Makie, Executive Vice President
> **Cambridge Industries**

"Short, to the point, and easy to read; I like the book very much."
> Stan Biga, Chief, Resource Development
> **Sikorsky Aircraft**

"Best overall explanation of the Toyota Production System."
> Tom Faust, Vice President GROWTTH
> **Freudenberg-NOK**

"Provides a great understanding of World Class Manufacturing as a strategic weapon."
John R. Black, Director, World Class Company Studies
Boeing Commercial Airplane Group

"An entertaining yet insightful look at an entire manufacturing process all the way from the design phase to ultimate customer delivery."
Harry Lewis, Vice President
Chrysler

"Teaches the Toyota Production System in a simple manner."
Rocco Losito, Corporate Director of Quality
LA-Z-BOY

"Excellent lesson in modern manufacturing systems for ALL employees."
Mervin Dunn, General Manager
Arvin Ride Control

"Teaches the basics of TQM and JIT in 45 minutes."
APICS

"Insightful - magic - easily understood and retained."
Mary Osmolski, Director, Stanley Production System
Stanley Works

"Explains the basic principles of modern manufacturing management."
Scott Gibson, Vice President
Castrol

"Great overview of World Class Manufacturing processes and techniques."
Jack Murrell, Vice President
ITT Defense & Electronics

"Innovative and interesting."
Michael Naylor, Senior Vice President
Rubbermaid

"All the key issues we face today in readable, concise and understandable form."
James D. Lang, Director of Technology
New Aircraft and Missile Products
McDonnell Douglas Aerospace

"Must reading for anybody manufacturing anything."
Bill Jasper, President
Dolby

"Simplest, most effective and still entertaining book I've read on principles of effective manufacturing."
Bill Shillingford, Plant Manager
Ford

"Easy read that makes a dynamic impact."
Bill DeMalia, Quality Manager
Solectron

"Illustrates the principles of 21st-century manufacturing."
Quality Progress

"Creates retained understanding of huge impact of creating and manufacturing a cost effective, quality product."
Ronald F. McKenna, Chief Operating Officer
Sundstrand Aerospace

M ALL I NEED TO KNOW ABOUT ANUFACTURING I LEARNED IN JOE'S GARAGE

World Class Manufacturing Made Simple

WILLIAM B. MILLER   VICKI L. SCHENK

♦ Bayrock Press ♦

Revised Edition
Copyright © 2004
William B. Miller   Vicki L. Schenk

Bayrock Press
(888) 670-7625
www.bayrockpress.com

ISBN 09630439-3-5

Printed in the U.S.A.

Table of Contents

A Journey Of A Thousand Miles Begins With A Single Step.

GETTING GOING

Saturday morning, early. The sun popped up over the horizon a couple of hours ago. A few high clouds are chasing each other across a clear sky. Should be a nice day for the project at Joe's house. Hope it doesn't get too hot.

Joe asked a bunch of people to help him build wooden shelves along the walls of his garage. Get a team together and do it all in one day, sort of like the last-century barn raisings. Mostly he asked neighbors, and their kids if they were old enough, from over in the prestigious River Oaks area where he lives. Me he asked because I work for him, about four levels down, at the Garrett Gear Company where he's Vice President of Manufacturing. Somebody he knows he can trust, I guess. I hope he's got his eye on me for some sort of promotion.

Joe said he had all the tools we'd need, so I didn't have anything to take but myself out to my old Pontiac parked at the curb. As I walked down the sloping concrete driveway, I spotted Ralph Morita leaving his house two doors down. Ralph's about my age. He and his family, a wife and two little kids, moved into the neighborhood a few months ago.

Ralph is employed at the facility Yamachi Gear opened across town from Garrett. I drove by it once to take a look. A lot of land, but only one building, probably 20,000 square feet. Too small to be any threat to Garrett.

When Ralph heard about Joe's shelf project, he asked if he could participate. Said he'd like to meet Joe and perhaps learn something from him since Ralph was going to have to get his garage organized one of these days. Of course, I checked with Joe, but that was like asking Sinatra if he minded if somebody watched him sing. Maybe better. It was like Babe Ruth asking Joe for batting tips. A Japanese wanted to learn something from an American!

On the way to Joe's house, Ralph and I chatted about the usual nonsense things that people do when they're acquaintances more than they are friends. We had what I call a "weedkiller and weather" relationship, named after the sorts of things that new neighbors talk about when they run into each other on the sidewalk. I didn't know many details about Ralph's personal or professional lives, nor he about mine. But he seemed like a bright articulate fellow (his English was sure a lot better than my Japanese!), and I was hoping that Joe's shelf project would provide an opportunity to get to know him better.

*Leadership Does Not
Demand Allegiance.*

Progress Requires Change;
If You Never Change,
You Will Never Progress.

PLANNING TO BUILD SHELVES

When we arrived at Joe's house, there were so many cars parked bumper-to-bumper along the shady tree-lined street that I wanted to kick myself for showing up last. However, three more cars arrived before Ralph and I made it to the double front doors of Joe's rambling rancher. In the kitchen, devouring Winchell's sugared and frosted goodies, I felt like I was at a casting call for a crowd scene in a movie. Were we going to build shelves or an entire house?

I pondered the matter through three chocolate doughnuts and one cinnamon twist, while the remaining neighbors arrived, then Joe called us all out to the garage. Joe is about six feet tall with gray hair and a weathered face that tells you he didn't learn about manufacturing while getting his M.B.A.. He stood two steps up on a sturdy ladder and addressed the group, which was spilling out to the driveway. We had close to twenty people, two-thirds adults up to middle age and the rest high school kids. Some of the kids obviously were attached to certain adults, and others looked like they'd been sent or recruited alone.

Joe explained that we were a large group, but that he wanted to "do it right." That's Joe, I said to myself. Gears or garage shelves, he believes in doing a quality job. I sneaked a look at Ralph, but I couldn't read his expression. I hoped he was impressed.

A sturdy workbench and tall white metal cabinets faced out from the back wall of the three-car detached garage, which also contained a door to the outside. The two side walls, sheetrock painted a light gray, were bare. Joe described his plan to build wooden shelves along them. On each wall would be four identical sections, each eight feet high by five feet wide, set side by side. The sections would resemble giant bookcases. Each section would have sides, top and bottom pieces, and six additional shelf planks, set at various vertical spacings to allow for storage of different-height items. The sections would be built individually in three subsections, like mini-bookcases, then assembled into complete sections and placed along the walls. Joe would paint them later when he had time.

The overall plan didn't seem too hard to grasp, and soon most of us were shuffling our feet or folding our arms, anxious to see the detailed drawings or plans and then get started. I noticed a few furrowed brows and inquisitive glances around the garage. I was puzzled until I realized these people were looking for the wood and the tools for building the shelves. Knowing Joe's penchant for neatness and security, I assumed the tools were in the metal cabinets. I didn't have a clue as to where the wood was. When I looked around the garage floor, I couldn't see anything more than bare concrete under a lot of scuffed work shoes and old tennies.

"Listen up!" Joe shouted, drawing my and everyone else's attention back to him. He waved a large thick brown envelope over his head while one of his sons — Russell, I think, who maybe was introduced to me once when he had a summer job at Garrett — passed out identical envelopes to everybody. Russ was a husky blond with his father's rough-hewn features and his mother's light coloring. He mumbled something as he handed envelopes to me and Ralph. I mumbled back something equally unintelligible, the traditional response to somebody whom you aren't sure you've met and whose name you aren't certain of.

Rustling of paper echoed as everybody opened the envelopes and looked at the material inside. Over the din Joe explained that he'd prevailed upon the Engineering and Manufacturing Engineering (ME) departments at Garrett to prepare a "first-class" package for the design and building of the garage shelves. Being from Garrett's ME department myself, I recognized most of the material. Engineering's contribution was threefold: drawings of the finished shelves; exploded views of the shelves, showing how the pieces would be fastened together; and lists of the components, from the wood itself (grade, color, and dimensions) to the screws to be used. Manufacturing Engineering, starting with Engineering's documents, had prepared written instructions of the actual manufacturing work to be done, from sawing and sanding the wood to final countersinking of the screws. They had prepared drawings illustrating how the three subsections would be constructed and then assembled together into a complete shelf section. It looked like a fine package to me, and I felt proud of Joe's decision to "do it right."

When I looked around the garage for confirmation of my feelings, I was jolted by several confused expressions. A couple of guys were down on their knees, examining drawings they'd laid on the floor. I watched them, and gradually it dawned on me that these people had never seen professional drawing packages before. There wasn't anything wrong with the package, it was simply over their heads. Well, they'll learn something today, I reasoned: they'll see how to perform a task in a thoroughly professional way! Then Ralph tapped me on the arm. He also seemed puzzled.

"Excuse me, Sandy," he said apologetically, "but I don't understand some of this information. It appears to be inconsistent." He showed me some differences between the Engineering and Manufacturing Engineering drawings. They were minor things like placement of screws and angle braces. I knew what my answer was going to be, but to be certain I spent a few minutes looking at the drawings. Finally I nodded confidently and explained the situation to Ralph.

"It's based on division of responsibility," I said. "Engineering designs the shelves, in the optimal fashion for performance according to customer specifications. Then ME — where I work — produces a manufacturing design. Maybe we standardize the inset for drill holes, to reduce setup time on a drill press. Or Engineering has used six different types of screws, but we can cut that to three by eliminating the smaller sizes: the savings in manufacturing time and procurement cost outweigh the tiny expense of using a larger screw than necessary. Or here's another example." I pointed at the drawings. "Since the shelf sections are going to be built in subsections, ME changed the placement of some of the angle braces in order to strengthen the subsections during construction and moving. They might even have added some braces." I started to count the angle braces on both sets of drawings.

"What does Engineering have to say about adding braces?" Ralph asked.

"Nothing," I laughed. "It's a manufacturing issue." Then, fearing he might misunderstand, I dropped the levity. "If there's any question, of course, we run something by Engineering to get their reaction. We only make changes that we know won't affect performance."

"Doesn't that add time?" Ralph asked. "I mean, if you have to go back through Engineering?"

"Sure," I replied, "but we want to get things right. Joe's a real stickler on that!"

"I see," he said, then he fumbled with the papers, rearranging them until he had the Engineering package in one hand and the ME package in the other.

"Does manufacturing need this for anything?" he asked, holding out the Engineering package.

"No," I said. "That's for Engineering's files. Manufacturing Engineering always produces the material for the production floor, even if they don't make any changes from Engineering's design. ME is always the information source and contact point for production."

Then understanding hit me like a tidal wave! I knew why Ralph and the others were confused. I sprinted to the front of the garage and spoke a few words to Joe. He stepped back up on his ladder and announced that the Engineering materials had been provided for our information and reference, but that all we would actually need today would be the Manufacturing Engineering drawings. Head bobs and murmurs of assent greeted this comment. People stuffed the unneeded Engineering materials back in the envelopes and tossed them on the floor or pressed them back into Russ's hands. Russ rapidly began to resemble a character from a 1930's slapstick movie who can't see where he's going over the stuff he's carrying.

"Let's do it!" somebody yelled. Joe pointed to the back door of the garage and announced that we would move the group to the back yard and get started. There was a ragged cheer, and the crowd started milling towards the door. Ralph hung back, so he and I were alone at the rear of the party.

"I was wondering," he said quietly, "if Garrett has ever considered combining the engineering groups. Design engineers and manufacturing engineers working together to create a product that satisfied the customer's requirements and could be efficiently manufactured. It would appear that such a combination could save much effort, time and paperwork."

"Wouldn't work," I said, shaking my head. "They live in different worlds. Engineers are *prima donnas*. Some have Ph.D.s. They want the perfect design, regardless of whether it's cost-effective or an average human being can actually produce it. We MEs are dirty-fingernails types. We go down on the production floor. You'd never catch an engineer in the factory, unless he was being a hero by helping out some poor dumb ME who didn't understand how to do what the engineer wanted. MEs don't go to Engineering, either, unless they want approval for a design change so the factory can make the damn thing!" I was a little surprised at my vehemence. So was Ralph.

"Why is there such conflict?" he asked. "Both departments are striving for the same thing, the good of the company. Why should they not work together?"

By that time we had made our way into the back yard of Joe's house. I was awestruck at what I saw and was interested in what Joe would have to say about it. I told Ralph we'd continue the engineering discussion later. Besides, what was I going to tell him? That people and things were what they were, and neither Ralph nor I could change them? I suspected he was probably not going to accept reasoning that wasn't more firmly grounded in logic. I would have to do some thinking. But I knew there was a rational explanation for two separate engineering departments apparently plowing some of the same ground. Half a century of American knowhow that had catapulted this country to be king of the industrial hill couldn't be wrong.

A Fool And His Inventory
Are Never Parted.

HOW TO BUILD SHELVES

Joe's back yard was huge, so big that the shimmering swimming pool and deck didn't seem to take up much space. What did take up a lot of space — probably a quarter of the half acre — was a tremendous pile of lumber. There seemed to be virtually all sizes and lengths of boards. It looked like mostly pine with some redwood thrown in. Sitting by the pile in a lounge chair that had been commandeered from the pool area was a rent-a-cop, complete with blue uniform, shiny badge, and nightstick. A table with papers stacked on it was beside him.

Joe was always thinking. Knowing the size of the back yard, he'd brought a portable megaphone outside with him. He stood in front of the lumber pile, slightly off to the side of the stone-faced guard, and faced our group.

"Listen up, everybody!" he bellowed. "We got some procedures to go over. I got a real good buy on this lumber, so I bought enough for some other projects I been considering doing around here. But that means we got to measure carefully and keep track of what we use, so I know what I got left. And I don't want a lot of small pieces of scrap that I can't use, so we got to be intelligent about how we cut the shelves and side pieces out of these boards. I hired Rocco here to make sure everybody fills out the proper paperwork when he takes a board. If you can't use the whole board, you also got to document it when you bring the cutoff piece back to the pile. If you don't, Rocco will break your kneecaps. Hah! Just kidding. Here, look at these forms and see if you got any questions." He put some forms in the hands of the people closest to him and asked them to pass them around.

As the paper was making its way back to us, Ralph said, "You know, Al's Lumberteria over on Seventeenth Street will cut lumber to length. They'll even deliver for free if the pieces are too big for your car or truck. I use them for all my home projects. I get quality service and ready-to-use lumber, they get all my business. It's a good arrangement for both of us. Do you suppose Joe knows about them?"

"I'm sure he does," I said confidently. "But Joe squeezes a nickel so tight George Washington screams. He got a good price on this lumber." I pointed to the pile.

"How much do you suppose will go to waste?" Ralph asked. "And what's the cost of keeping track of all of it? Security for it? Protecting it from the sun and rain? Al's Lumberteria has competitive prices. I've checked. They aren't making their money by charging me for service. Just the opposite. They provide the service and make money by knowing that I and other customers will come back. They run a phenomenal volume through their yard — spread their overhead over a lot of units. And their overhead doesn't include high inventory carrying costs. They buy from mills that run their operations the same way and deliver frequently. There's a ripple effect. Everybody wins."

I shrugged. There wasn't any point in arguing. Ralph simply didn't have the experience to appreciate what Joe was doing to keep his costs down. No wonder Yamachi Gear was only a small operation while Garrett was the big player in town in the gear game.

After the lumber inventory recordkeeping procedures were understood by everybody, Joe went on to explain the manufacturing process for the shelves. Russ had made seven cardboard signs, with the numbers 1 through 7 on them, and attached them to wooden stakes, which he drove into the ground in a large semicircle that covered most of the rest of the half acre. Joe walked out into the yard and stood by the sign numbered 4.

"Listen up!" Joe said through his megaphone. "We're setting this up like a real factory. The saws will be in area 1. We'll bring the wood over and cut it to the proper lengths. Then it'll move to area 2 for hand finish. Mostly sanding, of course. Area 3 will be an inspection station. From there the pieces of wood will split up and move to areas 4, 5, or 6, which will be the production areas for the three subsections that make up each complete section of shelving. Area 7 will be an inspection station for the subsections. Then the subsections will go to the garage for the final assembly crews to put them together on the walls. The garage will be called area 8. We'll cut and build in batches of two. That's a middle-of-the road batch size. It should keep things flowing while giving us some economies of scale. Any questions?"

A middle-aged man raised his hand. "Why is area 1 so far from the lumber pile? Can't we put the saws next to the wood?"

"Glad you asked that question, Ellis!" Joe boomed. "Never too old to learn. As you can see, the hand tools aren't out here yet. They're in the cabinets by the workbench in the garage. When we bring them out here, we'll need some controls over them — the drills, sanders, and so on. Not to mention the screws, sandpaper, rags, and other supplies. We'll put those in an area under Rocco's control next to the lumber and issue them out as they're needed. In manufacturing lingo, we call it a 'crib,' Ellis. Tool crib, for instance. We have to keep the production areas, like the saws, away from the controlled areas. You see?"

"I guess so," Ellis said in a subdued tone.

"Great!" Joe responded. "Any more questions? Okay! Let's everybody start divvying up according to your skills. Move over to the numbered area you're most comfortable with. If there's a crowd, move somewhere else. If you don't have any carpentry skills, you can be an inspector or a move person. You can't be the foreman. I'm the foreman!"

As I was pondering where I would best fit in, Joe whistled and pointed at me. "Sandy, take your friend and go into the garage. Help Russ bring out the tools. After we get started, you can go back to the garage. I need you in final assembly. That's where the rubber meets the road! You know how we do things at Garrett!"

When Ralph and I got into the garage, Russ was just beginning to unlock the cabinets and get out the tools, so we had a few minutes to wait until we could carry things to the back yard. I wondered if Ralph's reaction to Joe's outside production layout was any more positive than his reaction to the lumber inventory.

"Well, what do you think?" I asked him. "Pretty impressive, huh? Joe really knows how to lay out a production area."

Ralph stared at the floor for a few seconds. Then he looked up and said, "Sandy, I don't mean to offend you, but I am accustomed to doing things somewhat differently. I would have had precut boards delivered and stacked beside the driveway. I would have constructed the three subsections for each shelf section right here in the garage, then assembled the complete section and put it on the wall. A procedure that some of your manufacturing experts call *cellular manufacturing*, I believe. Each section would be finished before going on to the next.

"I would need two, perhaps three, other people to assist me. Movement of raw material and work-in-process would be virtually nonexistent. Movement doesn't add value. Waiting time doesn't add value. Everything that doesn't add value is waste. We don't want waste. Ideally every task flows directly into the next; sometimes tasks are even overlapped. At Yamachi we have a word for this flow without waste. We call it **nagara**.

"We would inspect our work as we went along. We would undoubtedly make minor changes in our process, perhaps even in the design, as we proceeded. We would learn to complement each other's skills, style, and speed, thereby achieving a high-throughput balanced production process. I would expect the eighth shelf section to be designed and built better and faster than the first." He paused as if considering how much more to say.

"Joe's approach is very different," he concluded. "I do not understand it, but I do not wish to prejudge it. So I will wait until the shelves are up to venture a final opinion. Will you allow me that courtesy?"

"You got it!" I said enthusiastically. "In fact, when we're done, if you don't admit that Joe's method was the best and most efficient, I'll buy you dinner some night next week at any restaurant you choose."

Ralph smiled and shook his head. "No, my friend, I can't let you do that unilaterally. But we can make a wager. You and I will continue to observe Joe's methods and discuss them throughout this day. We'll see the results when the shelves have been installed. If the methods were successful, then I'll buy you dinner. On the other hand, if you have changed your mind by that time, then you owe me a dinner. Fair?"

"You're on," I said. We shook hands on the bet, then helped Russ carry tools and supplies out to the back yard.

The Wise Do Only
What Needs To Be Done.

Complexity And Success
Go Together Like Oil And Water.

GETTING READY TO BUILD SHELVES

It took four trips between the garage and the back yard. As I trudged I vaguely noticed that another one of Joe's sons was setting up a computer on the glass-topped patio table outside the kitchen window, but I was too busy, trying not to drop my armful of tools, to pay much attention. Finally, Ralph and I had completed our chores and were resting while people ran extension cords from the outside outlets and familiarized themselves with the tools they were going to use. Other workers queued up for Rocco to issue them little plastic bags of screws of the various types to be used in production areas 4, 5, and 6. He filled the bags from the boxes the screws originally came in and meticulously wrote down the recipient of, and quantity in, each bag. He sternly instructed people to record all lost or damaged screws and reminded them to return to him for replacements. Ralph was intently watching the scenario, and an explanatory comment seemed appropriate.

"You may think that's a silly procedure," I said to him, "but it's the only way to know how many fasteners we use today."

"Not so," he replied after a little hesitation. "The drawings tell you how many are used per unit. Multiply that by the number of units you build. Deduct the total from the inventory."

I shook my head. "You can't detect loss that way. Scrap, pilferage, whatever. You have to carefully control and issue material. Record every transaction."

Ralph shrugged. "Different priorities. We focus on reducing waste, not recording it. Your company probably punishes people for reporting their waste. How are you ever going to get their help in reducing it?"

I snorted. "Everybody's honest? Not around here."

He shrugged again. "Not everybody. Enough so that the loss from the remainder doesn't have a significant financial impact. Which means you don't need a big system to record and report it. You have to identify and correct design and process errors that foster scrap, of course. That's part of a never-ending activity that we call *kaizen* — continual improvement. We collect and analyze data real-time, or as close to it as possible, in order to make improvements. Our goal is improvement, not big data bases, long reports, and precise accounting transactions. The difference sometimes can be subtle, but it's important."

I was thinking about how to respond to that comment when Joe bounded over to the patio table, where the young guy with the computer was sitting, and addressed the group through his megaphone.

"Listen up! This here is my oldest son, Joe Junior. Junior just graduated from State and started working in the Data Processing department at Garrett. Sorry, Junior, I forgot you call it *Information Systems*. Anyway, he's written a program on his computer here that will make life a lot easier for us today.

"Planning and control are the lifeblood of manufacturing. This computer is going to help us do both. It will print work orders for each batch of two subsection units. The work orders will show all the operations necessary to build the subsections, starting with cutting. The computer will assign unique numbers to the work orders. The work orders will travel with the units through the production areas. When the units leave an area, like area 2 — hand finish, somebody from the area will run over to Junior and give him a tearoff stub from the work order. Junior will put the data into his computer. We'll have a lot of activity here today, and this is the only way we'll be able to keep track of it.

"If we run into any problems, like defects noted during inspection, we'll put those into the computer. At any time we'll know both the location and status of every batch. That's control!"

"How about planning?" asked a tanned young lady who looked like she might be of college age. She was standing by the area 4 sign, so I guessed she was handy with a drill and screwdriver. "Are the printed work orders what you mean by planning?"

"Good question! The work orders will be printed according to a schedule. I've worked out approximate times that a batch should spend in each area. Allowing for setup and reporting time, I figure sawing should take ten minutes, hand finish five minutes, first inspection five minutes, each construction area fifteen minutes, and second inspection five minutes per subsection. We'll allow five minutes move time between areas, starting with moving the lumber to sawing. Standard move times make more sense than fine tuning them with a stopwatch.

"Since the construction areas work in parallel, total time for each batch will be eighty minutes. That includes moving the subsections into the garage. Remember that a batch is the six subsections for two shelf sections. For final assembly in the garage I've planned fifteen minutes for each shelf section, plus five minutes for touchup and final acceptance. Twenty minutes total." He consulted his watch. "We only have enough people for one assembly crew. That's good, two crews would just be running into each other. Eight sections times twenty minutes per is a hundred and sixty minutes for final assembly. Plus eighty minutes to pop the first batch of subsections out of the pipeline. Two hundred and forty minutes total. Four hours. It's now almost a quarter after ten. Let's say we're in full swing by ten-thirty. We'll be done by two-thirty, three o'clock if we take a half-hour lunch break. How's that for planning?"

Everybody, including the questioner, seemed to nod and murmur approvingly. I turned to Ralph and said, "Surely you can't find any fault with this. I admit, using computers on a back yard project might be overkill, but you sure can't say Joe isn't organized. And you have to admit, with his system he'll know what's going on at all times."

Ralph's face took on a bemused expression. "Sandy, if you were building one section at a time on the garage floor, you would know what was going on at all times. Without a reporting system and a computer. The large volume of work-in-process inventory in the back yard is why Joe needs his system. He'll continually have three or four batches of shelf sections in process, each batch at a different stage of completion. Each batch includes the components for *two* sections, which further increases the work-in-process inventory in comparison to building one section at a time. Of course Joe needs a system to keep track of it all. And with that volume flowing through his 'factory,' even the slightest unplanned act will ripple through everything else with a domino effect. So he'll need the ability to reschedule and juggle priorities on the fly. And he'll have to add some buffers to the operations and move times. Which he's done, you notice. After all, eighty minutes to cut and build six subsections for two shelf sections is a little high, don't you think?"

"Maybe," I agreed. "But the buffers don't hurt. They contribute to standardized scheduling. You can't schedule on a best-case basis. If you did, when problems occurred, you WOULD have a domino effect. With Joe's way, the steady flow is maintained. You have schedules you know you can meet. With the computer you can adjust intermediate schedules and preserve the final schedule, if you need to. Just wait and see — the system will work."

Ralph smiled patiently. "I'll wait. I agreed to that."

A second thought about the computer occurred to me. "Another advantage of using the computer is good records. Of what's been built, inspection results, and so forth. The computer is an essential tool of modern production management."

Ralph held up his hand in a traffic cop's Stop gesture. "I believe firmly in computers and other forms of automation. For many uses, including direct involvement in product design and the manufacturing process. Perhaps also in quality assurance, for example statistical analysis of defects. Recordkeeping sometimes is a useful function. I would enter into the computer information on completed and shipped units. But I would NOT use a computer to create unnecessary complexity and then create more computer systems to help me manage the complexity and analyze errors caused by the initial complexity.

"I would keep the planning systems simple, and I would not design complex systems for work-in-process tracking and reporting. Administrative complexity on the production floor adds no value to the product. It takes time and breeds errors, both of which generate increased production leadtime. Which generates more WIP, which adds to the complexity and to the error rate. Which seemingly generate a need for more systems. It's a never-ending cycle that is suspended only when the company runs out of patience or money to finance the WIP and expanded control systems. At that point, having achieved both high investment and high operating expense, the company limps along with nobody in top management, manufacturing, or information systems really satisfied with the results. Everybody is constantly under heavy pressure to meet their performance objectives. They may succeed in doing so, but not in the carefree manner they'd been promised. Things haven't really changed very much from the old days. Crisis management is still their dominant style. Be honest with me, Sandy. How smoothly do things really go at Garrett under Joe's leadership?"

"Ralph," I replied instantly, "some things will never change. I spend half of my days down on the production floor resolving problems. Purchasing is always expediting vendors, and the dispatch group is always changing work order priorities. And the last week of the month is always hectic. But we make our shipment schedule, almost every month. And the company is profitable, so I get my raise when review time comes around. Old man Garrett is happy, and so are the employees. How's Yamachi Gear? Is your company doing as well?"

"Actually," Ralph said, "Yamachi's worldwide market share is expanding at an annual rate of eight per cent. The unit volume growth rate is higher, because the overall market has been expanding. In contrast, your company's shipments have held constant or increased only slightly in most recent years. Garrett's profits haven't declined, because prices have remained high enough to cover cost increases. Your company sets prices to cover costs and add a profit margin. My company sells competitively, then reduces costs to make a profit. With its non-competitive prices, Garrett has actually been losing worldwide market share. Are you aware of that?"

What could I say? I wasn't. Matters like market share and product pricing are left for top executives at Garrett to discuss and worry about. Me, I just concern myself with getting out this month's production. And, today, with getting shelves built in Joe's garage. I said something noncommittal to Ralph, then turned my attention back to the situation at hand, to see what I had missed while Ralph and I had been talking.

Not much, it turned out. Junior was out in the yard, holding forth on his computer system for planning and tracking shelf production. People were passing around sheets of computer paper that I guessed were examples of work orders and schedules. I assumed they probably resembled their counterparts at Garrett. A few people had left their work areas to take a peek at Junior's computer screen. Joe was beaming, obviously proud of Junior, but not contributing much to the conversation. That was about what I'd expect. Joe was a big booster of computer systems, but he didn't actually know very much about them. He just knew that they were a necessary part of running a plant these days, and he knew which reports he was judged on and which ones he could use to judge his subordinates.

Eventually most of the people began to get restless. The bright sun was climbing the sky, and people were ready to do something before the midday heat hit. Joe could sense the mood.

"Listen up! It's time to start haulin', cuttin', and drillin'. Junior's going to run out the first batch of work orders. You've all got a few minutes to get a last cup of coffee and a doughnut. Then it's noses to the grindstone."

He grinned and stood with his hands on his hips. Joe loved to be in charge. People headed for the sliding glass door to the kitchen. Joe's coffee comment had given me an idea, so I walked over to where he was standing.

"Joe," I said, "how about an incentive plan here? I won't be needed in assembly for a while. I'll run to the store and get some soft drinks, beer and snacks. We can reward people who finish their tasks ahead of schedule. Give them a cold brew and a pleasant break before their next task. I'll put on a fresh pot of coffee for the caffeine junkies like me."

"Shit," Joe replied disgustedly. "An incentive plan? I'll give them an incentive plan, all right. Get their work done on time, and I'll stay off their asses! How's that for incentive? I'll tell you, Sandy, Junior's going to have current info in his computer on who's ahead and who's behind. I'm going to be all over the slackers like flies on horseshit. They'll have plenty of incentive, don't you worry!"

I went back to where Ralph was standing. The way Joe's voice carried, I assumed Ralph had heard the entire exchange. We walked to the garage, ostensibly to discuss final assembly, but also so I could cool off. Joe and I didn't see eye to eye on everything, I knew, but I had forgotten how tough he could be on people. And how proud he was of it.

"You don't have to say anything," I commented to Ralph when we were in the garage. "Joe doesn't believe much in positive reinforcement as a motivational strategy. He thinks people will screw off every chance they get. It's not the way I would do things, but what the hell — it's worked for him for a quarter of a century. He's probably not going to change now."

"No," Ralph agreed. "He probably isn't. It's too bad. He doesn't get the best out of people, does he? People don't like to work for him." The last was said matter-of-factly, without rancor.

"No," I admitted. "He doesn't, and they don't." I felt like I was betraying the company by saying that, so I tried to soften it. "Most of us try to concentrate on just doing our jobs well. And on where Joe excels, instead of on his deficiencies. He DOES know a lot about manufacturing."

"We'll know by three this afternoon, won't we?" Ralph said.

No Mistake Is Fatal
Unless You Make It So.

Fanatic: A Person Who Redoubles His Effort After Having Lost His Direction.

BUILDING SHELVES

We discussed the final assembly layout in the garage for a few minutes, but there really wasn't much to it. I started to wonder about Ralph's concept of simply building one shelf section at a time in the garage, but quickly put the notion out of my mind and led Ralph outside to see what was going on in the back yard.

What was going on was an odd mosaic of activity. The lumber movers and sawers were busy, but everybody else was just fiddling with their tools, preparing for the work to arrive at their areas. Ralph grabbed a chair from the pool area and sat down. I did so, too, although it felt strange to be sitting while others were working. I noticed that other people who had assigned themselves to final assembly were taking it easy, though, which made me feel better.

We watched the first batch of cut boards make its way through hand finish and then on to inspection. The inspectors picked up their tape measures, gauges, and squares to do their tasks while the movers, sawers, and sanders consulted their schedules to see when they were

supposed to move, cut, and finish the next batch of lumber.
I caught myself smiling involuntarily. I was pleased for Joe;
it was all working as he had planned.

I sat in my patio chair, enjoying the beautiful day,
admiring the clockwork precision of the scene before me.
For about five minutes. Then things started to go wrong.

One of the inspectors from area 3, a woman in her
mid-thirties, was becoming quite agitated. She was standing
in the sawing area, holding a board she had carried from
the inspection area. She was pointing to it and talking to
one of the sawmen, who seemed to remain calm. As I
watched, the sawman said something to her and shrugged
his shoulders, which REALLY upset the woman. Joe had
been functioning as a roving foreman. He had been jawing
in construction area 5, but now he hurried over to area 1.
He listened for about thirty seconds, then beckoned to me.
I hustled over to the area, accompanied by Ralph.

It wasn't actually much of a problem. Several of the
first batch of shelf planks had been sawed at angles not
exactly ninety degrees — some a bit more, some a bit less.
The miscuts were caused by the makeshift fixtures of big C
clamps on sawhorses, fixtures which sometimes didn't hold
the boards in exactly the right position. Well, that kind of
stuff is what I live for. I found some more clamps in the
garage, borrowed a square, spirit level and pencil from the
inspectors, checked out a couple more boards from Rocco,
and made some supplementary sawhorse fixtures with
guide boards marked so the operators could ensure a
ninety-degree cut. I showed them how to use the fixtures on

a couple of new shelf planks to replace the miscut ones, then I retired back to my chair with Joe's compliments ringing in my ears.

"That was a nice job," Ralph observed. "You're a good ME."

"Thanks," I said. "I'm usually pretty competent at troubleshooting."

"We call what you did *poka-yoke,* " he said. "Setting up a fixture, or any operation, so the work can be performed only one way — the correct way. In addition, your fixture is easy to use, with minimal setup. Another key concept."

I was learning a whole new vocabulary, I realized. Simple one-word descriptions of manufacturing concepts. I started building a mental dictionary of terms I had heard so far today: *nagara, kaizen, poka-yoke* . I was sure there would be more forthcoming.

"What do you suppose will be the next problem?" Ralph asked, interrupting my cataloging. I asked him what he meant.

"Think about the emphasis so far today," he replied. "Joe has focused on the planning and control systems. That's justifiable, to some degree. Managers are supposed to plan and control. But the manufacturing *process* is more important. How you're actually going to make an item efficiently with high quality. Tools. Training. And so forth. Joe's had Junior take the time to write computer programs, but has he asked you to evaluate the production process? It's only a matter of time until further mistakes are made. Probably a short time."

Ralph was right, of course, and Joe didn't object when I volunteered to spend time in each of the production areas, discussing the workers' tasks with them and offering suggestions for improvement. In each area I was able to make significant improvements over the ways people had been planning to do their tasks. The changes generally went smoothly. I tend to work with people, not boss them, and I've found that most people don't mind being shown a better way to do something. Especially if I'm willing to back down when I'm wrong or when something is just a matter of personal preference. Or when I point out a potential problem, but let them develop the solution themselves after acknowledging the problem.

Joe wasn't pleased about losing the time for my analysis, but he was philosophical about it. And he had a solution for the potential delay my work had caused. He grabbed the megaphone.

"Listen up, folks! We lost about forty-five minutes due to the miscut boards and Sandy's changes to our production procedures. But we've got Junior's computer, so we're going to prepare tighter schedules, taking about twelve minutes out of the time for each batch. Junior says the computer can distribute the decreased times across work orders according to a mathematical formula that optimizes total throughput. I get that right, Junior? The modified work order due times will keep us on our final completion schedule of three o'clock, even allowing for a lunch break."

"See?" I told Ralph. "It helped to have the buffer times in the schedule to counteract the effects of the mistakes and production process changes. The computer can create all the revised schedules, automatically. We won't lose any time, overall."

"That's one way to look at it," Ralph said cryptically. I didn't ask what he meant. I was afraid I'd be on the receiving end of another speech on doing things right, not redoing them.

Well, Junior cranked out more paper from his trusty computer and circulated it to the workers, collecting the old schedules and work orders in return. Some individuals weren't inclined to pay much attention to the new paperwork, but Junior was patient with them, explaining the revised priorities and task sequencing. Eventually people got over the interruption and settled back into their tasks. Production hummed along uneventfully for a while.

Until one of the hand drills broke. There were six drills being used, two in each of areas 4, 5, and 6, the subsection construction areas. Each area needed two drills since they were working with a batch, two shelf sections' worth of components. They needed bits, extension cords, chuck keys — the whole works. I was sure glad I wasn't paying for the tools; I was impressed that Joe actually owned six drills. I couldn't afford that many.

It was too bad he didn't own seven. The young lady from area 4 who had raised the planning issue with Joe called him over because her drill wasn't functioning properly. That led to Joe summoning me, of course. The symptom of the problem was intermittent operation: when the trigger was pressed, the drill would run, then stop, then run again, then stop, and so on. I quickly removed a few small Phillips-head screws, popped the case off, and looked for loose wires or short circuits. Without dismantling the drill, I couldn't see all the electrical connections, but the ones I could see were fine. I tried a different extension cord and wobbled the plugs a bit. No improvement.

"Could be a lot of things," I said to Joe. "I could take it all apart and still not find the problem." I pointed inside the pistol grip handle. "Example. The connection between the power cord and the interior wiring is totally sealed inside a rubber molding, then the handle halves are glued shut around it. If I break into the handle, I'll have to tape it up. You'll have the power drill equivalent of a kid's taped-up baseball after the cover has been ripped off. I don't want to be responsible for the safety implications of that."

Joe nodded in agreement. He learned his lesson on safety a couple of years ago when he ordered a worker to carry a large gear to the next work station instead of waiting for a fork lift truck. The guy hurt his back and dropped the gear, chipping a tooth off. A real "two-fer:" a customer order even further behind, and a good worker out indefinitely with a serious workmen's comp claim and potential lawsuit against the company.

"Nothing to do but split the lot," he said. Joe used the terms *lot* and *batch* interchangeably. "With only one drill, area 4 can't work parallel on two subsections. But with your help, Sandy, their work assignments can be revised. One team can drill, then another team can fasten while the first team drills the next subsection. One subsection will be finished first and can be sent on to inspection. Junior can calculate the schedules for the split lot so we don't lose any time overall. Some people are probably going to have to work a little faster, of course. Okay? Let's go!"

For the second time in thirty minutes, I restructured construction operations and Junior pumped the data into his computer. It spewed forth revised paperwork, including work orders for each subsection in the current and future lots that would be split as they entered area 4. Junior and I distributed and explained the paper. Since the workers now had a bit of experience with rescheduling, the exercise went more smoothly this time, and soon I was back in my patio chair, relaxing with a cup of coffee.

"Bad luck," I said to Ralph through a mouthful of chocolate doughnut that I had rescued from despair. ('Tis heartbreaking to see a few lonely doughnuts where once dozens had rested, and I always endeavored to do my best to relieve their loneliness.) "Why couldn't something break that we had spares of?"

"You had SIX drills," Ralph replied with a smile. "How many do you need?"

"One more." I grinned. "Whenever I use the last one. Of anything." Then I turned serious. "You'd think that a big investment in tools and equipment would reduce the incidence of key breakdowns. But it doesn't seem to. At least not enough."

"Why would it?" Ralph asked. "More equipment provides backup only if it remains as spare. If it's redundant. If you use it, you've actually INCREASED the probability of a problem. Statistically, the odds of something going wrong with one of six drills is higher than the odds of something going wrong with one of two drills. If you double the amount of equipment and tools in use, you must halve the failure rate simply to stay even."

I munched my doughnut and wiped chocolate frosting off my upper lip. Ralph certainly had a different way of looking at things.

"So you think investment in spare equipment is a good idea?" I asked. "Totally redundant equipment?" I wasn't dense enough to think that was his major point, but it was the only one I could argue against.

"You must have been a good debater in school," Ralph observed dryly. "I would stock a few critical spare components. Primarily, however, I would streamline the manufacturing process. 'Lean and mean,' as an ancient American expression once proclaimed. Work performed rapidly and *Just-in-Time* for use by the next worker.

"A high-leadtime high-inventory factory requires investment in more than the inventory itself and the racks and pallets on which it is stored. It requires increased investment in tools and equipment to work on it, and in trucks, cranes, and hoists to move it. More things to go wrong. As I am sure you know, things always go wrong."

"Amen," I said. "At least wherever I've worked."

"Everywhere," Ralph said. "Even at Yamachi, to some degree. Planning can be perfect — it's all theoretical. Execution can never be perfect — it involves real people using real tools on real material. All we can do is minimize the opportunities for imperfections, and the effects of them."

"Amen again," I said and stuffed the last piece of doughnut in my mouth. I wasn't sure I agreed fully with everything Ralph had said, but I was tired of raising futile arguments. I just wanted to finish my coffee in peace. And continue my vain wishing that Joe had owned seven drills. Then Joe's subsection building approach would have shone like polished diamonds, and I wouldn't have needed to argue with Ralph.

There's Never Time To Do A Job Right
But There's Always Time To Do It Over.

INSPECTING SHELVES

After I finished my coffee, I rounded up and briefed the final assembly crew in the garage. Ralph attended, but didn't have any comments, and he even wore a pleased expression when I had finished my explanation of assembly procedures. We returned to the back yard and our chairs to wait for a batch of subsections to pass through area 7, the inspection area preceding final assembly. I turned my mind off and attempted to relax. However, soon little alarm bells began going off in my brain, and I noticed that finished subsections were starting to jam up in area 7. I walked over to see what was happening, and I arrived there at the same time as a burly worker from area 6.

"What's going on here?" the worker said to the inspector in an aggrieved tone. "I can see you aren't sending any of our subsections on to Sandy for assembly. Is something the matter?"

"Something the matter?" mimicked the inspector, who was a short wiry man with iron gray hair cut in a military flattop. "Yeah, something's the matter! None of the screws are countersunk properly. They're too deep. The wood putty Joe puts over them when he goes to paint will dry unevenly and crack. I'm rejecting the whole lot."

"From all of areas 4, 5, and 6?" the worker asked incredulously. "You don't think anybody countersunk the screws correctly?" He turned to me. "Sandy, the drawings show a countersink depth about the thickness of a screw head. That's what we tried to do. Isn't that okay?"

Flattop didn't give me a chance to answer. "I don't give a rat's ass about what Ol' Sandy says! I'm the inspector here, and I say these don't pass! Go back and do them again!"

The worker silently handed me the drawings. It didn't take long for me to see that a difference of opinion was possible. The drawings showed just what the worker said, but they lacked precise notations of both countersink depths and inspection standards, i.e. allowable variances.

I tried to speak calmly. "Uh, it looks like you both may be right. The drawings illustrate countersinking, but they aren't precise on either the depth or inspection standards. There evidently was an oversight. Now that the depth is an issue, we can discuss it and..."

Flattop whirled to face me. "Horse puckey! I worked twenty years in QC, and I don't listen to no ME. Or anybody in manufacturing. QC reports directly to the President. How I interpret drawings is solely my decision, and I say the countersinks are too deep! Fix them!"

"Fix them yourself, asshole!" the worker said. He turned his back and strode away, passing Joe who had been discussing something with Russ, but now was coming over to investigate the raised voices. The worker quickly disappeared around the side of the house, and I knew we wouldn't see any more of him today.

Joe worked out a compromise whereby the inspector would pass the subsections already built and the workers henceforth would countersink screws to lesser depth. I thought it was a tactful solution, and I said so to Ralph as we headed to the garage for the first final assembly.

"I suppose so," Ralph replied. "I'm not that familiar with confrontational inspectors. At Yamachi, people are expected to inspect their own work, both for function and to specification. We have formal inspection departments only when it's required by your government contracts or a special expertise is involved such as using a laser gauge. Workers are an integral part of quality. Statistical and analytical charts are maintained on the production floor by workers, not by Quality Assurance people in a remote office. Workers are proud of their work. It's considered poor form to pass on a defective part and wait for someone else to detect it. Similarly, nobody can arbitrarily call somebody else's work defective. If there's a question, the parties involved discuss it and reach a resolution."

"What if they don't agree?" I asked. "What if each person sticks to his position?"

Ralph shot me a piercing look. "We don't permit personal egos to dominate. We do what's best for the customer. In the rare cases when disagreement still exists, somebody will give in so as to avoid further wasted time. We encourage a culture where getting on with productive work is valued more highly than disruptively 'sticking to one's guns,' I think it's called. I admit it's more difficult with an American work force, but we've had a great deal of success. It's my opinion that confrontation isn't a native part of most American workers' and managers' psyches. It's simply how they've learned to behave. But you prove to them they'll benefit more by cooperating than fighting, and they'll cooperate. Who wouldn't? In Japan, many companies average more than twenty suggestions per person annually, with an implementation rate of over ninety percent. That's *Total Quality Management* — everybody in the company participating in improving quality!"

The move people had moved into the garage the six subsections for the first two shelf sections. The assembly crew was waiting for directions, so I tabled my thoughts about responding to Ralph. Not that I had anything particularly brilliant to say. The idea of eliminating "confrontational inspectors" had blown me away. What were inspectors supposed to be if not confrontational?

Quality Is Not A Spectator Sport.

*Moving Fast Is Not The
Same As Going Somewhere.*

FIRST ASSEMBLY

The time was quickly approaching half past 12:00. Joe called everybody from the back yard to be on hand to witness assembly of the first section of shelves from its three subsections. It was a nice gesture, giving the workers an opportunity to see the results of their labors.

People were spread out across the driveway, arrayed in front of the garage like zoo visitors observing the orangutan playpen. Most of them were sweaty and looked as though they appreciated the break. As they had passed by me, I had heard a muttered comment about forming a union. I guess Joe heard it, too, because he announced that we'd take a short lunch after the first section was up on the wall. Unfortunately, he went on to say that if they didn't take the full half hour, they'd be able to make up most of the time they were spending idly on the driveway instead of being in the back yard performing their production tasks. Just his way of paying somebody back for the union comment, I supposed, but it sure killed the effectiveness of the break and his gesture.

I had marked on the concrete floor the locations of the front corners of the bottom subsections. We planned to assemble each entire section, then lift it into place. However, cautious person that I am, I wanted to test the locations. I set the first two bottom sections in their places against the wall, the front corners nudging the crossed lines of my chalked X's.

They rocked. Both of them. Only slightly, but they rocked. Joe had designed the shelves with the bottom shelf plank to run flat along the floor. A similar piece ran horizontally at the top of the shelves. The vertical side pieces were attached by long screws through the top and bottom pieces into the end grain of the vertical pieces. The interior shelf planks were then attached by screws through the side pieces into the ends of the planks; they were also secured by angle braces. The design had at least two major things going for it. One, the vertical fastening of the top and bottom planks made the whole section less susceptible to side-to-side swaying. Two, the bottom plank flat on the floor removed a potential dust and dirt trap under the shelves.

Unfortunately, the garage floor wasn't perfectly flat. It was flat to the eye, but the bottom planks were sensitive to the slightest undulation and bump in the concrete. I knew when both bottom sections rocked that the problem couldn't be warped bottom boards, but we checked them with levels and squares, anyway. No dice — the boards were perfectly flat. Too bad the floor wasn't.

The fix was pretty obvious. Take off the bottom board, shorten it, and reinstall it between the side pieces like any other shelf. Set it maybe half an inch up from the bottom, and let Joe buy some weatherstripping later to seal the half-inch space from dust and dirt. I described the fix to Joe. He wasn't smiling, but he nodded. Grimly. I'd seen that look on his face before. It was his expression when he hated taking the time to do what had to be done, but recognized that further discussion — looking for a miracle — would result only in further delay. The man didn't cry over spilt milk; he cleaned it up and moved on. Certainly one of the things I admired about him.

So we tested the fix on one of the bottom sections, the one that wobbled the most. It worked. The section sat as solidly as the Washington Monument. No reason to believe the fix would fail, of course, but it wouldn't have been the first time in my life I had missed something in my analysis. Anyway, I hadn't missed anything this time. I started to work on the second unit, but Joe interrupted me.

"Let the other guys fix that unit," he said. "We've got a bigger problem." He gestured towards the back yard, and I realized what he meant. Six other bottom subsections were out there in various stages of completion. In every one, the bottom plank was cut to the wrong length, and most subsections were further along in construction than just having the boards cut. We'd have to identify and fix each subsection in place before allowing it to proceed. Junior could print out a computer listing that would tell us the exact progress of each affected subsection. Joe asked me to help him work with the people to make corrections. "Just like your normal ME floor liaison job, Sandy." It was, but I was understaffed here. Joe agreed when I suggested I could use Ralph to help me.

"I'll have to cancel lunch break," was Joe's final comment. "Otherwise we'll never fix the remaining bottom subsections and finish final assembly by three o'clock." I just shrugged. Missing lunch to implement engineering changes in production was hardly a foreign concept to me. Not that it often happened on weekends in somebody's garage, however.

While Joe broke the news to the workers, Ralph and I headed for the back yard to see Junior. He wasn't yet aware of the problem. Like most computer people would have, he had stayed close to his electronic toy rather than come to the garage to watch the production operation. Systems people like everything about manufacturing except having to actually do it or get too close to it.

"I suppose you're going to tell me this wouldn't have happened with your approach," I said to Ralph after we were out of Joe's hearing.

"You don't need me to tell you that," he replied. "Joe's padded schedules and inflated work-in-process mean that a part or subassembly problem discovered in final assembly causes a LOT of problems further upstream. Problems equate to waste, which must be eliminated. I believe in building the finished product as rapidly as possible. You'll find out fast if there are problems with it, and you'll minimize the number of in-process units that are affected. The best idea is to use every part or subassembly in its next higher item as soon as possible after it's built. That's the quickest way to identify and correct errors — be they product, process, human, or equipment errors. We call that **jidoka** — immediate feedback on a defective item, before more defective items can be produced. Correcting process deficiencies is vital — it prevents future waste. We will bring all resources required to bear on a problem. I'm sure you've heard of the famous **andon** system, whereby workers use flashing lights or other means to signal a problem that must be fixed before production can resume."

I nodded. "I know about it." And didn't say that I once heard Joe comment that workers being able to stop production was the dumbest thing he'd ever heard of and sounded like Communism to him.

Ralph went on. "The best method for ensuring that you can use a part immediately after it's built is not to build it until it's absolutely needed. Not according to a theoretical schedule, according to which you PUSH material and work orders into production. But according to a real need that PULLS a part or subassembly into the next operation. Using real live people in production who communicate their needs with empty containers, **kanban** cards, or something else."

"A computer?" I asked, somewhat hopefully.

"Perhaps," Ralph answered. "Kanban originally referred to an identification tag on a container designed to hold a fixed number of parts. It can be any document that notifies an operation that the subsequent operation is out of parts, as when an empty container is sent to a producing operation. Computer-generated documents are fine if they communicate real needs, not theoretical needs. In an actual factory here on planet Earth, real needs are not the same as needs computed from master schedules and bills of material. Things happen — customer order changes, engineering changes, inventory corrections, process improvements. You simply can't lock yourself into an imaginary future that may not occur. Not only because bad things can happen, but also because you don't want to preclude good things from happening. For instance, what does Garrett do when an engineer comes up with a product improvement — to cost or functionality? Unless it's a mandatory change — like a safety issue — the company breaks in the change at the point of a future work order release. If there are ten work orders in process, you can't change those. So ten batches or items get built without the improvement. Right?"

"Yes," I said. "That's the way it works. Most of the time. Usually changing the design in the middle of production would negate the value of the improvement, at least for the in-process items."

"Correct!" Ralph said patiently. "So you want to have fewer in-process items. Think of your factory as a garden hose attached to a faucet. Material and labor enter one end, and finished goods shoot out the nozzle. New customer orders and most engineering changes are input at the faucet end. They travel through the entire hose. The longer the hose, the longer they take to exit out the nozzle. Yet the *output rate* from the nozzle doesn't change. A long hose and a short hose both yield the same flow from the nozzle, the same output rate for finished goods. But there's a big difference in how long it takes for a drop of water to get from the faucet TO the nozzle."

"Unless I turn up the water pressure," I replied, somewhat maliciously. Ralph wasn't fazed.

"Every analogy has its limits," he said, "but how often does increasing the pressure have more benefits than drawbacks? Perhaps in washing dirt off your driveway. Not if you're watering delicate plants. And what do you do when you've reached maximum safe pressure? There's a limit to what higher pressure can accomplish before the hose ruptures."

"Tell that to Sales," I said cynically. "They sell half of their orders with compressed leadtimes, then yell at manufacturing to produce them on time."

"They're responding to the market and competition," Ralph said. "Customer delivery requirements drive production cycle time requirements. Perhaps modifications to your manufacturing approach could reduce production time and improve Garrett's competitive position."

"Maybe," I said grudgingly. I didn't want to admit it, but I was starting to understand the benefits of a low-inventory, short-leadtime approach to manufacturing. I wondered if Joe would be amenable if I presented it to him in the right way.

However, by then we were standing by the computer table on the patio, so I set the thought on my mental back burner while I explained our situation to Junior. Whatever his other traits, he wasn't dumb or slow, and pretty soon Ralph and I were into the production areas, pulling out the partially completed subsections that required corrections. I marked them with masking tape and a red felt tip pen so they would receive high priority. Joe joined us shortly, accompanied by the workers themselves. Nobody looked happy, but there was a clear attitude of determination. Within moments the air was filled with the sounds of sawing and disassembly in addition to the drilling and fastening noises from the continued construction of the unaffected middle and top subsections.

The Finest Carver
Does The Least Cutting.

*You Can Fool Some Of The Customers
All The Time And All Of The Customers
Some Of The Time, But You Can't
Fool All The Customers All The Time.*

ASSEMBLY — AGAIN

With the changes to the bottom shelf planks, final assembly proceeded smoothly. At Joe's suggestion, I had maintained my strictly supervisory role, in case any further problems arose. They didn't, unless you count the fact that the three o'clock target wasn't going to be met. The final assembly crew was functioning so well that I was spending most of my time monitoring the remaining activities in the back yard. However, the plain fact was that my digital watch had just displayed a line of 2s. Although the subsections would be completed in time, the assembly crew had just finished one wall and simply wouldn't be able to assemble the other four complete sections in the thirty-eight minutes remaining. I thought.

But I underestimated Joe. He was still wearing his grim **I-won't-be-defeated** look when he walked over to me.

"Subsections be done in the next ten minutes?" he snapped.

"All but two sections' worth done now," I answered. "The rest are almost ready for inspection. The bottleneck is final assembly in the garage — the crew can't handle this big a load dumped on them instead of flowed in evenly."

"The sawers, sanders, and area 3 inspectors want to go home," he said. "They think they're tired and hungry. I told them to hang around. I want you to pick the best of them for assembly. Two full crews in total, working fast, starting immediately. We'll be done in half an hour."

"I don't know, Joe," I said hesitantly. "They aren't trained. They might make mistakes, or – "

"Dammit, Sandy!" he exploded. "How hard can it be to put shelves together! You watch them, make sure they do it right. Just get it done! I don't miss schedules making gears, and I'm not going to miss them making garage shelves!"

Well, I didn't fancy arguing with Joe any more on Saturday than on Monday through Friday, so I did what he wanted. I left Ralph in charge of getting the remaining subsections through inspection, and I cobbled together a second final assembly crew. I watched and advised them throughout every minute of their work, not even casting an eye towards the first crew. I knew from seeing the first crew's work up on one wall that they didn't need any supervision. The second crew was a different story, but nobody ever tried harder under pressure. They didn't panic even when the first crew had completed their work, and the full glare of Joe's spotlight was on them as three o'clock drew steadily closer. By that time of course all the back yard work had been completed, so the assemblers had an audience of Joe, Ralph and some of the subsection constructors. I didn't envy them.

When they stepped back after placing the final section on the chalk marks, I made a quick check of the fit and tightness of the shelves and the smoothness of the surfaces. Fine. I shot Joe a thumbs-up signal and looked at my watch. It said 2:56. I mouthed the words '*four minutes*' to Joe. He tapped his watch and nodded, already composing his victory speech in his head.

At that moment Ralph said, "I think they're crooked."All eyes swung to Ralph, then to the shelves. He was right. The two sections assembled by the second crew were leaning very slightly — one to the left, and one to the right. The slanting would have been unnoticeable except for the fact that the adjoining units were straight as a plumb line. The tiny gaps between the straight and slanting units stood out like the Grand Canyon.

A member of the first final assembly crew spoke up. "Even though the bottom sections don't rock any more, the floor still isn't perfectly horizontal. We did a little sanding on the bottoms of the vertical pieces until the spirit level showed us that they were standing at a true ninety degrees. I guess the second crew didn't know about that. Or Sandy. We were too busy with our own work to pay attention to what the second crew was doing. Sorry."

I looked at my watch. Two minutes to three. Well, I conceded, that's what happens when you're spread too thin. I couldn't simultaneously monitor back yard production and both assembly crews. Some days you eat the bear, and some days the bear eats you.

Suddenly Joe roared, "WE'LL SHIM THOSE SUCKERS!" He reached under the workbench and picked a handful of wood shavings out of the waste barrel. He pressed them into my hands while yelling "PUT A LEVEL AGAINST THE UNIT! NOW!" to the speaker from the first crew. The guy was startled, but he moved like he had a red S on his chest. He pulled a spirit level from his back pocket and slammed it up against the side of one of the leaning units. Joe rocked the unit while I pushed chips under the short leg with a screwdriver blade. We did the two shelf sections faster than you could say quick-and-dirty. When I stood up and checked my watch, the main readout said 3:00 and the seconds indicator had just flashed 51.

"It's three o'clock for nine more seconds yet, Joe," I said. "We made it."

He smiled his executive smile of happiness but no warmth. "Never a doubt, Sandy. A man is capable of whatever he thinks he is. That's how we make schedule at the plant, and it's how we made it here today." He turned to face the rest of the group, which at this point was down to about a third of its original size. Only a couple of individuals from the back yard, other than the ones I had conscripted, had stuck around for the final act of the drama. The rest had departed.

"I want to thank you all," Joe said. "I'm sorry I can't invite you to hang around for a beer, but Virginia and I need to be at the club for a social function later this afternoon. We'll have you all over for dinner sometime soon. Watch your heads now. I'm going to close the garage door." We hastily cleared out of the garage as Joe walked towards the back of the garage and stabbed a button mounted on the jamb of the outside door.

*Darkness Is Merely The Period
Before The Dawn Of A New Day.*

GOING HOME

Both Ralph and I were silent until I had started the car and pulled away from the curb. Then he looked at me and said, "Very educational day. Thanks for inviting me."

"You're welcome," I replied. A couple of blocks later, "I think I owe you a dinner."

"Only if you're sure," Ralph said.

"I'm sure. That last-minute performance with the shims was just too much. Made me realize how much product we ship exactly that way. Joe's very proud of his on-time shipment record. Yet we never have an easy time making schedule. We're under the gun almost every month. We cut corners continually, and every month we ship at least a couple of gear assemblies that technically passed final inspection, but that I wouldn't like if I were the customer.

"We achieve this marvelous performance with so many people they're falling over each other and pallets of inventory stacked in front of every one of our numerous expensive computer-controlled machines. You know why things happen that way? I think I finally figured it out."

"I believe so," Ralph said. "But tell me."

"Because we make things hard for ourselves. We don't do things the sensible way. We spend money and effort focusing on the wrong things, while we ignore the basics. I've learned more about manufacturing from you today than I have in eight years at Garrett."

"Thank you, Sandy," he replied after a few moments. "If you'd ever like to consider helping Yamachi make gears, please give me a call."

"I'll do that," I said. "Now, how about we go to my place and grab that beer that Joe wanted so badly to give us, but didn't have the time."

"I accept your offer," Ralph said. "I think it's time we got to know each other better.

THE END

*You Must Give Up The Present
To Have The Future.*

*Life Is A Story
For Which You Write
Your Own Ending.*

EPILOGUE

Yamachi Gear was a pretty good place to work. I learned a lot, and I was also able to contribute to the plant's success and thereby to the well-being of my fellow workers and managers, ninety percent of whom were Americans. One of my better efforts is on the following page, an attempt to distill into a few words the things I have learned about attaining manufacturing excellence.

*A Society That Venerates Shoddy
Philosophy And Scorns Good Plumbing
Will Have Neither Philosophies Nor
Pipes That Hold Water.*

TEN COMMANDMENTS OF MANUFACTURING EXCELLENCE

1. **PULL** production stingily through the factory pipeline instead of mindlessly pushing material and labor into it.

2. **BUILD** and **SHIP** rapidly to improve manufacturing productivity, rather than storing and moving inventory.

3. **SQUEEZE TIME** out of the cycle from order receipt through shipment by eliminating redundant tasks and tasks that do not contribute directly to output or quality.

4. **IMPROVE** product design to enhance manufacturability and provide increased functionality and reliability to the customer.

5. **REDUCE** per-unit consumption of purchased material and supplies.

6. **REFINE** the production process to promote simplicity and decrease resource consumption.

7. **IDENTIFY** and **ELIMINATE** manufacturing errors at point of commission.

8. **SIMPLIFY** information and control systems; integrate them efficiently with design and production.

9. **COOPERATE** and **COORDINATE** with suppliers and service providers to share knowledge and increase joint effectiveness.

10. **STRIVE** continually for incremental improvements in all activities involved with design and delivery of the product to the customer.

*What Is Well Planted
Cannot Be Uprooted.*

GLOSSARY

After I had worked with Ralph for a while, my mental dictionary of new words and phrases had grown considerably. For the benefit of new workers at Yamachi, one day I put down on paper the following definitions. (If you're reading this, Ralph, I DO remember that you mentioned I had missed the nuances of some of the Japanese words; I hope you remember we agreed that, for introductory purposes, a simple definition that was 90% correct was preferable to a lengthy treatise that was 99% correct.)

andon:
a system of flashing lights used to indicate production status in one or more work centers; the number of lights and their possible colors can vary, even by work center within a plant; however, the traditional colors and their meanings are:

green:	no problems
yellow:	situation requires attention
red:	production stopped; attention urgently needed

AQL:
abbreviation for Acceptable Quality Level, an outmoded concept which holds that there is some non-zero level of permissible defects.

autonomation:
in Toyota parlance, automation with a human touch; English translation of jidoka — please refer to glossary entry for jidoka.

cellular manufacturing:
an approach in which manufacturing work centers [cells] have the total capabilities needed to produce an item or group of similar items; contrasts to setting up work centers on the basis of similar equipment or capabilities, in which case items must move among multiple work centers before they are completed; the term **group technology** is sometimes used to distinguish cells that produce a relatively large family [group] of similar items.

fishbone chart:
a diagram that resembles a fish skeleton, with a main spine and branches [bones] drawn at a slant off the spine; used for quality control in two main ways:

1. as a cause-and-effect diagram, where the spine denotes an effect and the branches are cause factors

2. as a subdivision of quality requirements, where the spine represents a quality objective and the branches describe subsidiary traits or measurements that are important but are not the end in themselves

flexible manufacturing system:
an integrated manufacturing capability to produce small numbers of a great variety of items at low unit cost; a FMS is also characterized by low changeover time and rapid response time.

Ishikawa diagram:
a name for the fishbone chart that recognizes its developer, Kaoru Ishikawa.

jidoka:
A Japanese word which translates as autonomation; a form of automation in which machinery automatically inspects each item after producing it, ceasing production and notifying humans if a defect is detected; Toyota expands the meaning of jidoka to include the responsibility of all workers to function similarly, i.e. to check every item produced and to make no more if a defect is detected, until the cause of the defect has been identified and corrected.

Just-In-Time:
a production scheduling concept that calls for any item needed at a production operation — whether raw material, finished item, or anything in between — to be produced and available precisely when needed, neither a moment earlier nor a moment later.

kaizen:
the philosophy of continual improvement, that every process can and should be continually evaluated and improved in terms of time required, resources used, resultant quality, and other aspects relevant to the process.

kanban:
a card or sheet used to authorize production or movement of an item; when fully implemented, kanban (the plural is the same as the singular) operate according to the following rules:

1. all production and movement of parts and material take place only as required by a downstream operation, i.e. all manufacturing and procurement are ultimately driven by the requirements of final assembly or the equivalent.

2. the specific tool which authorizes production or movement is called a kanban. The word literally means card or sign, but it can legitimately refer to a container or other authorizing device. Kanban have various formats and content as appropriate for their usage; for example, a kanban for a vendor is different than a kanban for an internal machining operation.

3. The quantity authorized per individual kanban is minimal, ideally one. The number of circulating or available kanban for an item is determined by the demand rate for the item and the time required to produce or acquire more. This number generally is established and remains unchanged unless demand or other circumstances are altered dramatically; in this way inventory is kept under control while production is forced to keep pace with shipment volume. A routine exception to this rule is that managers and workers are continually exhorted to improve their processes and thereby reduce the number of kanban required.

lean production:
an English phrase coined to summarize Japanese manufacturing techniques, especially as exemplified by Toyota.

line balancing:
equalizing cycle times [productive capacity, assuming 100% capacity utilization] for relatively small units of the manufacturing process, through proper assignment of workers and machines; ensures smooth production flow.

minus-cost principle:
a principle of establishing reasonable and necessary cost targets through subtraction of required profit margins from the prices necessary to generate desired sales volume and market share; contrasts with the opposite approach of adding margins to costs in order to establish selling prices; the term reflects the reality that profits, which are prices minus costs, can only be improved permanently through cost reductions.

mixed-model production:
capability to produce a variety of models, that in fact differ in labor and material content, on the same production line; allows for efficient utilization of resources while providing rapid response to marketplace demands.

nagara:
smooth production flow, ideally one piece at a time, characterized by synchronization [balancing] of production processes and maximum utilization of available time, including overlapping of operations where practical.

poka-yoke:
a manufacturing technique of preventing mistakes by designing the manufacturing process, equipment, and tools so that an operation literally cannot be performed incorrectly; an attempt to perform incorrectly, as well as being prevented, is usually met with a warning signal of some sort; the term poka-yoke is sometimes used to signify a system where only a warning is provided.

pull system:
a manufacturing planning system based on communication of actual real-time needs from downstream operations — ultimately final assembly or the equivalent — as opposed to a push system which schedules upstream operations according to theoretical downstream results based on a plan which may not be current.

setup time:
work required to change over a machine or process from one item or operation to the next item or operation; can be divided into two types:

1.   internal: setup work that can be done only when the machine or process is not actively engaged in production; OR

2.   external: setup work that can be done concurrently with the machine or process performing production duties.

shojinka:
continually optimizing the number of workers in a work center to meet the type and volume of demand imposed on the work center; shojinka requires:

- workers trained in multiple disciplines;

- work center layout, such as U-shaped or circular, that supports a variable number of workers performing the tasks in the layout;

- the capability to vary the manufacturing process as appropriate to fit the demand profile.

SMED:
abbreviation for Single Minute Exchange of Die; literally, changing a die on a forming or stamping machine in a minute or less; broadly, the ability to perform any setup activity in a minute or less of machine or process downtime; the key to doing this is frequently the capability to convert internal setup time to external setup time; variations on SMED include:

1. Single-digit setup: performing a setup activity in a single digit number of minutes, i.e. fewer than ten.

2. OTED: One Touch Exchange of Die; literally, changing a die with one physical motion such as pushing a button; broadly, an extremely simple procedure for performing a setup activity.

SQC:
abbreviation for Statistical Quality Control; using statistical methods to identify, prioritize, and correct elements of the manufacturing process that detract from high quality; proper SQC is NOT the use of statistical methods, such as sampling, to ensure that defects are kept below an acceptable level; refer to AQL in this glossary.

TQC/TQM:
abbreviations for Total Quality Control and Total Quality Management; "Total" refers to:

1. a company-wide emphasis on quality, including all individuals and all functions.

2. an examination of all aspects of the company's processes that design, sell, produce, deliver, and service items for customers.

waste:
activities and results to be eliminated; within manufacturing, categories of waste, according to Shigeo Shingo, include:

1. Excess production and early production.
2. Delays.
3. Movement and transport.
4. Poor process design.
5. Inventory.
6. Inefficient performance of a process.
7. Making defective items.

5S:

refers to five words *seiri, seiton, seiso, seiketsu, shitsuke.* These words are shorthand expressions for principles of maintaining an effective efficient workplace:

seiri:	eliminating everything not required for the work being performed
seiton:	efficient placement and arrangement of equipment and material
seiso:	tidiness and cleanliness
seiketsu:	ongoing, standardized, continually improving *seiri, seiton, seiso*
shitsuke:	discipline with leadership

Like many concepts, the 5S can be interpreted narrowly or broadly, depending on circumstances of their use.

Success Is A Matter Of Luck;
Just Ask Any Failure.

ADDITIONAL READING

When I asked Ralph for written material on the manufacturing techniques he favored, he gave me the following list and commentary. "The list isn't exhaustive," he cautioned; "there are certainly good books that aren't on the list. However, these will get you pointed in the right direction." He added that his primary criteria for inclusion of a book on the list were that the book dealt explicitly with tough manufacturing issues; that specifics of implementation and operation were spelled out; and that the book reflected hands-on experience in real companies. He also noted that most of the books were truly original, not regurgitations of somebody else's material.

Costanza, John R.
Quantum Leap: In Speed to Market
Several editions

Comment: a broad view of world class manufacturing from an American perspective; discussion of "Demand Flow Technology" (a kind of pull system) and quality control as key elements; includes business functions other than pure manufacturing, e.g. product design and finance.

Goddard, Walter E.
Just-in-Time: Surviving by Breaking Tradition
Several editions

Comment: an overview of new manufacturing approaches (broader than Just-in-Time); includes experiences of several U.S. companies; describes marriage of Japanese and U.S. manufacturing techniques.

Hirano, Hiroyuki
5 Pillars of the Visual Workplace: The Sourcebook for 5S Implementation
Portland, OR: Productivity Press, 1995

Comment: this is a well-done translation of Hirano's Japanese edition; highly readable, the book clearly explains each of the 5S in detail, and provides concrete advice for implementation, including specific action steps.

Imai, Masaaki
Kaizen (Ky'zen): The Key to Japan's Competitive Success
New York, NY: McGraw-Hill Publishing Company, 1989

Comment: explains kaizen, the philosophy of continual improvement; includes numerous case studies; discusses the management and practice of kaizen, including implementation and changes in a company's culture.

Ishikawa, Kaoru
What is Total Quality Control? The Japanese Way
Several editions

Comment: a prescription for high quality, prepared by the individual recognized as perhaps Japan's foremost quality guru; describes both concepts and specific methods.

Monden, Yasuhiro
Toyota Production System
Several editions

Comment: a detailed description of the world's most effective and efficient manufacturing system, the system which best exemplifies Japanese manufacturing techniques.

Schonberger, Richard J.
Japanese Manufacturing Techniques: Nine Hidden Lessons in Simplicity
Several editions
World Class Manufacturing: The Lessons of Simplicity Applied
Several editions

Comment: an American analysis and interpretation of key elements of the best Japanese manufacturing; includes Just-in-Time, Total Quality Control, and other elements; the second book builds on the first; both books discuss some examples of implementation in the U.S.

Shingo, Shigeo
Non-Stock Production: The Shingo System for Continuous Improvement
Several editions

Comment: a lengthy discussion, with examples, of the concepts of Japanese production management; stresses clear thinking and underlying reasons for actions − "know-why" in addition to "know-how;" discusses the transition from the "Authorized Stock Production Era" to the "Non-Stock Production Era."

A Study of the Toyota Production System From an Industrial Engineering Viewpoint
Several editions

Comment: another detailed look at the Toyota system, including its conceptual underpinnings.

Zero Quality Control: Source Inspection and the Poka-Yoke System
Several editions

Comment: an excellent discussion of: management functions regarding quality; inspection systems; use and design of poka-yoke approaches; over 120 pages of specific examples of poka-yoke methods.

*Give Not To The Teacher
Responsibility For The Learning.*

*The Easiest Way
At First Seems Hard.*

Final Thoughts

To many readers, as to us, Joe and the events in his garage are only TOO real. We must confess, however, that we made up the whole thing. The characters, companies, names and all other details are fictional. Any perceived resemblance to specific real individuals, businesses, etc., is strictly a product of the reader's excellent imagination.

Most of the philosophical sayings are original. The remainder are sayings that, in one form or another, have been around for a long time, but a specific unique source is unknown and indeterminable, at least to us. If any reader has a different idea, please share it with us. You can contact us through Bayrock Press at the address on the order form.

The cover graphics were designed by Rina Dion. If you think the cover is as good as we do, and you would like to contact Ms. Dion, you can do so through Bayrock Press.

Bill Miller   Vicki Schenk

Act Without Agitation;
Strive Without Strain.

About The Authors

Bill Miller and Vicki Schenk are principals of W. Miller & Co., a management consulting firm that assists manufacturing companies. Their experience ranges from turnarounds of troubled companies to strategic implementation of *Value Based Manufacturing*®, the next generation beyond World Class Manufacturing. They are familiar with virtually all products and processes, from delicate medical instruments to automobiles and aircraft, from metal fabrication to electronics assembly. Their clients include public and private companies of all sizes.

Bill Miller has run manufacturing companies and served as a partner of an international management consulting firm. His earlier book *America's Management Challenge* was a selection of the Executive Book Club. Vicki Schenk is a veteran consultant and manufacturing executive. She has held senior operations and engineering positions, including Chief Operating Officer, for startup and mature companies.

W. Miller & Co. can be contacted through their website www.wmillerco.com.

*The Tranquil Is Master
Of The Turbulent.*